The Heart of the Matter

Barbara Griffith

The Heart of the Matter

AuthorHouse™
1663 Liberty Drive
Bloomington, IN 47403
www.authorhouse.com
Phone: 1 (800) 839-8640

Published by AuthorHouse 11/30/2018

ISBN: 978-1-5462-6517-7 (sc)
ISBN: 978-1-5462-6518-4 (e)
ISBN: 978-1-5462-6519-1 (hc)

Library of Congress Control Number: 2018912612

Print information available on the last page.

authorHOUSE®

The Heart of the Matter

Dedication

Thank you to everyone who has shown me love, friendship, kindness and support. It has been a journey! Special thanks to my family for loving me through thick and thin.. and for not giving up on me for my persistence in this creative endeavor.

To my children, Cote, Calle and Jack .. may you always love and be loved and look for the heart in everything......I promise you, it is there. Love, Mom

Acknowledgements

Designed and written by:
Barbara Griffith
Coronado, California

Photography by:
Barbara Griffith

Belle Mitchell
Belle Mitchell Photography
http://www.CoronadoBelle.com
Coronado, CA

Gracie Smith - Artist
Coronado Art on Canvas
Coronado, CA

Lydia Perkins - Pastry Chef
Sweet Lydia's of San Diego
San Diego, CA

AuthorHouse Publishing
Karen Stansberry
Myra Baldwin
Leigh Allen
Bloomington, IN

You can see a heart in everything; just tilt your head for a better view.

A puzzled heart is always looking for the perfect piece.

Hope and Intrigue

A heart should remind you to stay focused and keep looking for your peace.

You pass through life but once; you pass through others' hearts eternally.

Harmony

Valentine's Day should be celebrated every minute of every day.

Isn't it the best day when you hear "I love you too"?

Love is a verb. What action are you going to take to get it?

Love is the finish line; make that the goal you are aiming for.

Joy

Paint your heart on the easel of life and use all the colors.

Jewels and gems belong in a treasure chest; love is
the treasure that belongs in the heart.

Devotion

A beautiful soul will always be a beautiful heart.

Passion is not a four letter word; delight in it.

Forgiveness

If you tend your own garden in life, your heart will bloom.

Cupid, the God of Love, strikes unexpectedly and remains in the heart forever.

Friendship

Love does not come and go, it stays in the heart forever.

Create

Your heart is porous. Let it breathe....

When you believe in love, you will thrive in love - so let your heart soar!

Comfort

You are mine and I am yours; the words to last a lifetime.

Don't wake up and sing alone; go out and sing with the choir.

Gratitude

Wherever you go, there will always be love around you; embrace it.

The heart of a mother is where you will always find forgiveness.

Love and Happiness

Dissect your heart and see what you can find; it will be amazing.

Love can demand a certain outcome; so let your heart pound louder.

Sincerity

There has never been a heart as big as yours.

Try not to break a heart for someday yours may be broken.

Delight

Do not jeopardize your soul as it contains your heart.

Love, hope and passion are intertwined to fill your heart.

Compassion

Self-expression should be accepted by all hearts.

Never question your heart; it most likely has the answer.

Mystery
Strength
Adventure

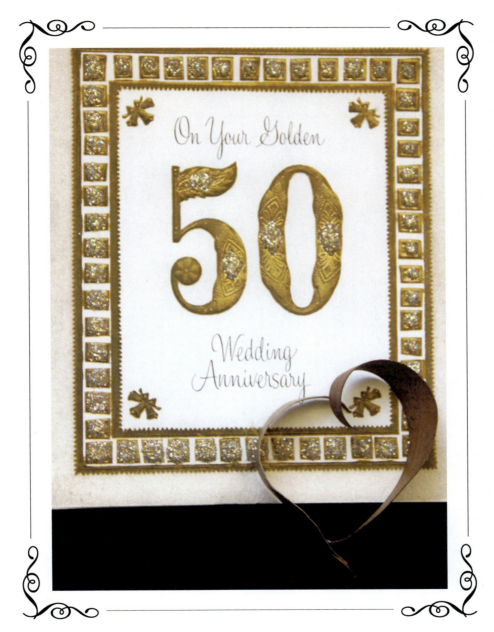

Romance

The kitchen is a perfect place to produce love...

...it shows up as comfort food.

Imagination

The heart is always under construction; look for a great contractor.

The purpose in life is to always keep your heart beating.

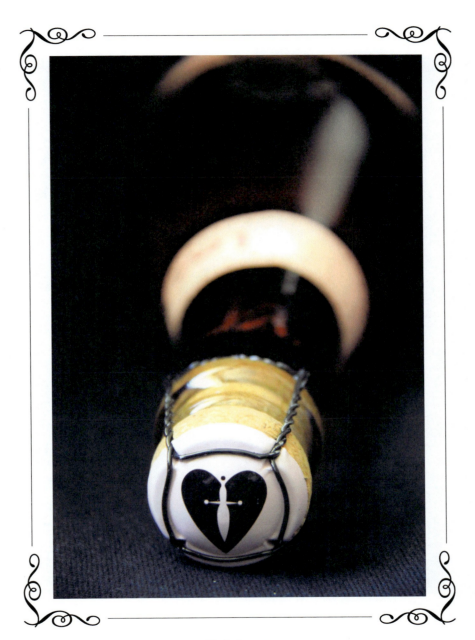

Celebrate

Happiness is an emotional response that comes from the heart.

It is extraordinary and wonderful to never let your feet touch the ground. Sit a spell and feel your heart beating.

Strength in life is given by the pumping of your heart.

Whose heart is more open and free than that of a child?

Peace....Honor....Dedication....and Love....

Your past does not define your future ... Look for the heart
in everything and let your story begin.......